The full beauty of the rose is already present in the bud—
Swami Radha at age 19.

the rose ceremony

swami sivananda radha

TIMELESS BOOKS

- PO Box 3543, Spokane, WA 99220-3543
  509-838-6652 or 1-800-251-9273

- In Canada: Timeless Books, Box 9, Kootenay Bay, BC V0B 1X0
  250-227-9224 or 1-800-661-8711

- In England: Timeless Books, 7 Roper Rd., Canterbury, Kent CT2 7EH
  (011-44) 1227-768813

First Printing March 1997; Second Printing August 1997

Edited by Swami Gopalananda

Design by Clea McDougall

Printed at Yasodhara Ashram, B.C., Canada

Published by

Table of Contents

part 1 Entering the Symbol

part 2 The Ritual

part 2 continued

'God, here is a flower. I have not made the flower. I have no power to create a flower. I have really nothing, not a single thing, I can call my own. But I take this little part of your creation, and I give it back to you, charged with my love, my emotions, and my devotion. Please accept my offering.'

—Swami Radha

part one

Entering the Symbol

Preface
The Hidden Power of the Rose
Swami Gopalananda

You are about to embark on a ceremonial journey into the heart of a symbol. If you allow yourself to enter the temple of your imagination as you read these pages, the ceremony will start to come to life for you. You will also gain considerable insight into the power inherent in a symbol, in this case the beautiful rose.

The seed for the Rose Ceremony was planted many years ago during Swami Radha's time in India. She often saw rose petals being used in the worship of Divine Mother and in Pada Puja (worship at the feet of the Guru). Although she

was personally reluctant to emphasize the ceremonial or ritu-
alistic aspects of worship, she saw that a simple ritual could be a
means for expressing the very fine feelings that can emerge from
gratitude and humility. One day in Dehra Dun, where she had
been sent by her Guru, Swami Sivananda, to learn Indian dance,
she spontaneously created a little rose-offering ritual to him
out of a deep feeling of gratitude for all that he had given to her.
Back in the West, when she was asked by some of her Catholic
devotees if there was a ceremony they could incorporate into
yoga that would honor the Virgin Mother, it was quite natural
for her to respond from her experiences in India. From this
early impetus, her ideas for the Rose Ceremony began to take
form.

With the Rose Ceremony, Swami Radha has created an
original way for us to make a personal commitment or dedication to an ideal. Revelation of the beauty and power of the ceremony rests entirely in how each of us experiences the process.
Elaborate or simple, the purpose of the ceremony remains the
same—to create a means for remembering. Sincerity is the key
to your experience of the Rose Ceremony; you have to be willing to be touched by the **process in the** same way that you would

–swami radha–

want to be touched in any interaction with a beloved.

The following pages describe the different symbolic aspects of the Rose Ceremony as they would appear during an actual ceremony. Swami Radha's commentary in each section is composed from several Rose Ceremony talks she gave over the years. The reflections throughout the text are drawn mostly from my own experience. The questions posed in the reflections can serve as a starting place for your own journey into the ceremony.

Introduction
The Origins of the Rose Ceremony
Swami Radha

"**G**uru! It's Saturday. Where's the chocolate?"

The young man stood in front of me obviously quite angry. I had never been addressed by him in such a demanding tone before, and I could not understand what was going on with him.

"Don't you know?" he said. "Haven't I told you already? May is the month when the Virgin Mother is celebrated as the Queen of the Roses."

So that was it. No, I did not know. I was still very new in my work in the West, and I had not wanted to meddle in the traditional beliefs of those people who were coming to me to learn about yoga. But clearly this young man expected something from me—perhaps a way for him to build a bridge between the Eastern and Western traditions of Divine Mother. What could I do? I had not come from a religious background, and I was quite skeptical about rituals.

My mind went back to what I knew from my experience in India, and some things began to come together for me in a way that they had not before. As I made the connections for myself, I could begin to see the form that a Rose Ceremony might take as a bridge between traditions. But such a ceremony could also build a bridge to Divine Mother according to what she represents within each of us. Ramakrishna did this with a prayer to Divine Mother that he repeated on each bead of his mala. He would take one bead at a time and say to Divine Mother, particularly in the form of Kali, "I give you my health and my sickness; give me divine love. I give you my wealth and my poverty; give me divine love." He would say this prayer for all the polarities he could think of in the range of human emotions. I was very impressed hearing about this, having visited the Ramakrishna Order in Calcutta and having had a terrific

–swami radha–

experience there in Ramakrishna's own room on the grounds of the Kali Temple. My recollection of his prayer was a good beginning.

Just before leaving India, I was in Kailas Ashram, which is the starting point for the pilgrimage to Mt. Kailas, legendary home of the ice-cave abode of Lord Siva. The leader of Kailas Ashram knew I was leaving in a few days, and he looked at me very seriously, nodding his head, and then he turned to another fellow and said to him, "Get all the rose petals from the morning worship of Divine Mother and give them to her." The young disciple went to the temple, picked up a whole bunch of rose petals, knotted them into a good piece of cloth, and gave them to me. And then the head of the Ashram said to me (he always had his mala in his hand), "Every day I will give you one round of the mala to support your work. There will be many blessings for you in the work for the West." Then he looked at me very seriously and continued, "It will be very difficult, very difficult. At this moment you cannot even envision how hard it will be. But don't worry, you are protected." As I look back, I can see that he was a person of great wisdom.

The first flowers I bought for my Guru, Swami Sivananda,

– *rose ceremony* –

at the bazaar in Rishikesh were roses. When I returned to the
Ashram, I saw that the thorns on the roses could injure him, so
I removed them all before giving the flowers to him. When I
handed the roses to him, he put his hand out to accept them,
and then suddenly he pulled his hand back. "The thorns!" he
said.

"There aren't any," I replied. "I have removed the thorns so
that you wouldn't be hurt."

"Ah!" he said, "you understand."

But I must be frank, I did not understand. My actions were
done simply out of consideration for him; if I brought something to him or did something for him, I felt that it should not
make pain, period. That was my attitude at the time. A few days
later he said to me, "Divine Mother will take away many thorns
from your life." All this happened quite some time before I went
to Kailas Ashram and had the experience I've already mentioned.

In India, following my initiation into sanyas on the 2nd of
February, 1956, I had the experience of the Light that I've de-
scribed in the *Divine Light Invocation* book[1] and the *Radha*

book.[2] From that experience I began to think, Now I know what Light is. But I wondered, How has this Light created me, and what was I the last time?

A few years later I was visiting some people who have a wonderful property in Vancouver, and I heard a beautiful songbird.

"What is it?" I asked.

"We must have a nightingale here," they said, "unless it is a canary that has escaped its cage."

And that remark, "the bird that has escaped its cage," stayed with me. Several years later, at a particular time when I was being bombarded by psychologists who were unable to measure (according to their standards) what I was doing to develop my mind, I said to them, "Look! Stop trying to ridicule and humiliate me just because you're wanting a sparrow. I'm very happy to be a canary. I chant the Mantra *Hari Om* at least two hours a day, and I've done that for five years. Now I suggest you do the same for yourself and see what happens." After that episode the idea of the canary escaping its cage began to make sense to me.

Now I shall make a small leap here. I asked myself, How can I put some of these experiences together into a ceremony with the rose? I thought if I remove the petals, each one representing a pair of opposites, and place them into a bowl of water asking for divine love in return, that would be one way. And the center of the flower is like the hub of the wheel; all the petals are attached to the hub. If I take the center and put it into the water with the rose petals, then perhaps that could be a way to make the suggestion to myself that I can become one with my own inner Light. If I am not a sparrow, but a canary, as I claimed, how could the canary become one with the rose? And from this line of thinking I wrote a poem:

Many old gods are still around
wearing different garbs
and masks as times are changing
self-importance grows
authorities' impact intensifies

The rose looks impressive
Thorns are big and sharp
tiny ones stick in the skin
The nightingale sings
its last song.

This poem has to do with what I had long observed about the established religions: so many splintered sects each with its priests thinking that what they had was the best and only way. But as the centuries go by, all that changes, even within their own denominations.

Having experienced the rose as one, but also the perfume of the rose as one, I wanted to have that oneness that doesn't change—a rose remains a rose. I had to ask, How can I get to that place in myself, knowing that the established religions cannot help. Then the image of the bird came back to me. The nightingale in the poem, pressing its little chest against the thorn, realizes that unless it gives everything it has—its life—to the rose, it can never be one with the rose.

The poem, of course, is metaphor; the rose grows at the entrance to a secret place on the moon, and the moon is symbolic for the mind. But the moon also represents the reflective function of mind because it has no light of its own. The moon reflects the sun. In the same way, we have no wisdom of our own unless we open ourselves up to find the map to that secret place in our own mind where not just light per se is reflected, but where *all* Light is reflected.

I think you can see from my own experience with the rose that there can be considerable power in a symbol. And, of course, building a ceremony around the symbol led me to think much more deeply into my own experience, which was a real confirmation for me of the path of freedom I had chosen. The nightingale definitely has a song different from the sparrow's chirping, although the sparrow has its own sweetness, for sure. There's nothing dreadful or shameful in being a sparrow. But there must also be room for the nightingale.

[1] Swami Sivananda Radha, *The Divine Light Invocation,* (Spokane: Timeless Books, 1990).

[2] Swami Sivananda Radha, *Radha: Diary of a Woman's Search,* (Spokane: Timeless Books, 1981).

Symbol
Gateway to the Other Side of Mind
Swami Radha

Your own unfolding is like that of the rose. First there is a seed that has to germinate and put out roots. All of this takes place beneath the soil, long before you can actually see anything happening. The roots grow deeper into the ground to get a firm hold and to get nourishment. Where are your roots in this life? What are you rooted in? These are important questions to think about.

Next, a little green shoot, very tender, breaks through the soil and into the light. After the shoot has grown a little more, the first two leaves appear. They are coarse, but the leaves that come after are more and more refined, until finally the first bud appears. As the bud slowly expands, the flower begins to emerge, until one day it is fully open. I think of this symbol of the rose as a lovely metaphor for your own growth, and eventual spiritual unfolding.

Symbolism is linked with thought association, and in this particular ceremony we have a very rich and meaningful symbolism. The Rose Ceremony is a means of guiding your thinking, your interpretation, and eventually your understanding into greater depth. Interpreting symbols according to your personal experience can reveal the depth of knowledge and experience that is already in you. Symbols, like scripture or inspired poetry, expand your capacity for understanding—sometimes I call it the light of understanding. Your interpretation and experience of a symbol is the starting place to that deeper understanding. The symbolism of the Rose Ceremony is an opening for you into your own thinking.

–swami radha–

The Symbols Used in the Ceremony

- Two glass vases, each containing an equal number of roses
- A glass or crystal bowl filled with water
- Two candles
- Fire
- Prasad—sweetness
- Scissors

Ceremony
The Means to Remember
Swami Radha

*I*ndia has a lot of very lovely rituals dedicated to Divine Mother, and it was after seeing some of them that I was able to bring ideas for the Rose Ceremony back to the West. According to our Christian background, Mary, whom we also call the Queen of Heaven, is our form of Divine Mother. In the East, Divine Mother is called Shakti, the creator of all that is manifest. In India it is recognized that all power manifest comes from the one source. In other words, the power and its manifestation are inseparable. By way of illustration we could say the flower and the scent in the flower are inseparable. You can't separate one from the other. And so each one of you, male and female, is inseparable from the divine power. To help establish that idea in your mind, the Rose Ceremony is both a dedication and an acceptance of that power at the same time.

On the other side, you cannot have a personal relationship with a power that is impersonal to you. Once that power manifests, you can love the power in its manifestation. But you can only have cosmic consciousness if you have accepted Divine Mother's creations in all her forms, not just the beautiful and the satisfying. Only if you accept all creation will you have access to that very special place that you call cosmic consciousness. That consciousness is signified by the dot in the centre of the Sri Yantra where all the triangles finally meet.

The decision to do the Rose Ceremony is, of course, a very special one. In order to make it you must clearly see the questions before you: Do you want to be rooted in the pursuit of something that gives you some satisfaction and a place in the world, or do you want to be rooted in divine love? Nothing grows without being rooted in something. By doing the ceremony for yourself, you make a decision about where you want to be rooted in this life, and that is very important. Such a decision will follow you throughout your life.

In the case of the Rose Ceremony, the questions are concerned with ideals and the purpose of life: Why was I born? Why am I here? What am I planning to do? How do I see my life? To begin to answer such questions, we have to make our priorities clear, and that means starting to make decisions. Sometimes priorities may overlap or be so close together that a decision may be rather difficult to make. It is important to understand, however, that making a decision strengthens us. Even if we make a wrong decision in life, we can learn from our mistakes. Courage and willingness to take a stand come from that learning.

The ceremony itself is your dedication to the Most High. You have two vases, each filled with roses. One vase is dedicated to the Most High, to God; the other is dedicated to yourself. The ceremony is your means to dedicate yourself to the Most High. It is not a promise to me or even to the Ashram. It is your promise to the Most High. However, it is not one of

those ceremonies or initiations that are for the rest of your life.
The Rose Ceremony can be repeated. Next year when roses
bloom again, you can repeat it. If you feel a need for it, you can
repeat it sooner. This is all up to you. It is your decision. But
even a temporary dedication can make a great deal of difference
in your life. You know where you are going.

How To Do a Rose Ceremony
Swami Gopalananda

*C*reating a special atmosphere to honour a dedication ceremony is important. If you are doing the ceremony at home it can be held anywhere in your house that you have designated to be special or sacred. Chanting a Mantra or having a quiet period of meditation before beginning the ceremony will help create a receptive atmosphere, particularly in your own mind. Most important is the care that you put into your ceremony; that care will influence the effect considerably.

You'll need two vases of roses on your altar, one containing enough roses for everyone taking part in the ceremony and the other containing an equal number of roses as an offering to Divine Mother. Your altar should have two candles, as well.

Everyone together can start chanting a Mantra, usually *Hari Om,* the healing Mantra. Chanting continues throughout the first part of the ceremony. When you are ready to begin your dedication, you go to the altar to receive your rose. You then return to the bowl of water with your rose and begin to remove the petals one by one, placing them one at a time into the water. As you do this you repeat softly to yourself the pair of opposites represented by the petal—love and hate, sickness and health, selfishness and generosity, anger and compassion, to name a few—and ask for divine love in return. Making a list beforehand of the opposites that you feel are active in your own life helps to bring your attention to their interplay in your mind.

When all the petals have been removed, you are left with the centre of the rose, where all the opposites were attached. It is now time to show yourself the degree of dedication you feel you are ready to make. At this point you can cut the stem with scissors, leaving the centre of the rose attached to the stem, and place the cut pieces beside the bowl. Or you can cut the centre of the rose from the stem and place it into the bowl along with the petals. Both actions reflect a degree of commitment, and the decision is entirely yours.

–swami radha–

The first part of the ceremony ends when everyone has presented his or her own rose to the water. The *Hari Om* Mantra that you've been chanting together from the beginning of the ceremony will slowly come to an end in its own natural time, after the last person has completed his or her dedication. You can leave the petals in the water overnight, but you'll need to allow time for them to dry before the second part of the ceremony. Before sleep, make a list of your grudges and resentments. Happily, in the second part of the ceremony you'll be burning them up along with the dried petals and leaves. Finally, try to keep some quiet time and privacy for yourself between this part of the ceremony and the next.

In the second part of the ceremony, you'll need prasad (a special sweet made for the celebration), a small ladle for distributing water, and two small containers. You'll also need a fireplace or other suitable spot to build a fire. Make the fire before starting the ceremony to allow time for it to become good and hot, and have the tray of leaves, stems, and dried petals from the night before close by the fire.

This part of the ceremony also starts with chanting a Mantra, this time to Lord Siva, Remover of Obstacles. When the fire is ready, each person in her own time can go to it with her list of grudges and resentments and put the list into the fire, along with a handful of petals, leaves, and stems, to be consumed once and for all in the fire of wisdom. Chant *Om Namah Sivaya* vigorously as the flames transform the dross and residue into a new beginning.

To end the ceremony everyone chants together while a sip of water from the bowl of rose petals is given to each participant. Prasad is given out next, and the ceremony ends with chanting a prayer or by repeating the *Divine Light Invocation* Mantra together. Later, after the fire has cooled, come back with your little containers and collect some of the ash and some of the rose water. The ash will remind you that once old resentments are burned to ash, they ought to remain so and not be resurrected anew. The water you can have any time you feel a need for it. You'll be surprised at how fresh it tastes, even months after the ceremony.

Reflection

I enter the Temple, take my place, and begin my
Rose Ceremony. Soft chanting fills the space that
I occupy, and after a minute I join in. My voice,
tremulous at first, becomes stronger as the Light
fills my mind. I realize for the first time that it is
the temple of my own mind that I have entered. I
am happy to be here now. It feels as if I am
taking a stand for my own life. That would
explain the tears welling up. Does the soul cry?
What a surprise! I did not expect to feel this way.
Perhaps the tears can be offered back too.

—Swami Gopalananda

part two

The Ritual

Candlelight. Soft, warm, steady, unassuming—
even a tiny bit of light is powerful enough to
dispel darkness. The Divine Light Invocation
given to us by Swami Radha promises to change
forever the darkness of a poor self-image. My
mind reflects any image it focuses upon until that
image manifests in my life. My mind has no light
of its own; it must reflect the light from another
Source. Yet the light itself is neutral. Do I really
understand the awesome power of choice?

—Swami Gopalananda

Candle

—Swami Radha

The two candles represent your two selves: the physical, material self that is tied up with all the personality aspects and your Higher Self. Each candle is sustained by the same light. But where there is light, there is also shadow. My physical body obstructs the light, creating a shadow, but my shadow does not have a life of its own separate from my body. The energy, which is neutral, creates both and comes from the same source. The material-physical and the mental-spiritual all exist by the power that comes from the one source. So let not this division that you sometimes feel stand in the way. My shadow and I are not really separate. The underlying energy of life is the same even though that energy manifests in many different ways.

The rose I am given is beautiful. Everything, even the most exquisite beauty, lasts for only a moment. Is there anything that endures? Something must, otherwise death would have no purpose.

I take my rose to the bowl of water, kneel, and begin to remove the petals—removing the illusions one by one, looking for the real and the lasting.

—Swami Gopalananda

Rose

—Swami Radha

The rose is a most beautiful flower, sometimes called the queen of the flowers, and it commands all of your senses. Eyesight participates by being enchanted with the beauty of the rose, and you can feel the velvety softness of the rose petal between your fingers. The perfume of the rose travels through the air. Can you see it? No. Spiritual perfume travels, too, and some people with a good sense of smell can perceive the spiritual perfume from another person. The rose is satisfying to your sight, emotions, touch, smell, and even to your taste. Rose oil is used in marzipan, the paste made from almonds. Rose oil is very precious. Many pounds of rose petals are needed for just one drop of oil.

Many people associate roses with love. For each of us the word *love* has a particular meaning, and it is good to clarify for yourself what you mean by it. For example, when do you call an emotion love? If you help a couple to stay together for the sake of their children, is that love? Or is it compassion for the children's future? When does love become so impersonal that you're willing to help under any circumstances? It's hard to say. Perhaps the best thing is not to think so much about love, but to develop instead a high degree of concern and consideration for others.

Why do we use red roses in the ceremony? Red is the color of blood, the very life force itself. You can live without food and you can live without a lot of comfort, but if you were drained of the last drop of blood, your brain would collapse. There would be no more thought—however divine—not even a prayer. Red stands for life, and life has to be accepted, not denied. By accepting the give and take of life in the proper sense, and by establishing your ideals, you enrich yourself and make your life worth living. When you have done this, you have little or no

–swami radha–

fear of death because you know you are doing your best. Life is then seen as most precious because each time we come into a life we are given another chance. It is God's love that gives us the opportunity again and again to keep on trying.

As I place each petal into the water I think of the miracle I have found: a purpose for living, far removed from the perpetual play of opposites I had assumed to be real. I place each pair of opposites into the water—love and pain, sickness and health, joy and sadness, wealth and poverty (it's good there are a lot of petals)—and with each I ask for divine love in return. I can begin to trust the durability of that love.

—Swami Gopalananda

Petals
—*Swami Radha*

The centre of the rose is the sun, and the petals are the infinite but harmonious diversities of Nature. Our nature is made up of personality aspects and the force of opposites which are represented in the rose by the petals. As you remove each petal, you think of it as representing a pair of opposites, and you offer that to the Divine asking for love in return: "I offer my knowledge and ignorance, and I ask for divine love in return. I offer the positive and the negative in myself, and I ask for love. I give all my feelings of love, all my feelings of hate, and all the degrees in between, and I ask for divine love in return." We could have the world with all its wealth and power, but if we did not have love, we would be very, very poor. It is in giving—in the true giving of ourselves and in the true sharing of whatever we have—that we receive.

It is the play of opposites in us that creates never-ending conflict. This continual movement between the opposites means I am constantly going back and forth between punishment and reward. Now I give them to the Divine, because in the past I have not handled the resulting conflict very well. When we re-move the petals in the way that we do (as an offering to the Most High) then the work of transformation is given direction and a next step.

—swami radha—

Spine consciousness is such an integral part of yoga. What does it mean to be spine conscious? The most beautiful part of the rose cannot live without the stem. From darkness to light, from earth to heaven, what is it that creates and briefly sustains this momentary flash of radiance that is consciousness itself? What is my connection to That?

—Swami Gopalananda

Stem
—Swami Radha

The rose you are holding in your hands is like the body. The stem represents the spine and the rose is the head. A spine that is light and straight (but not inflexible) can be an indication that one's thinking is straightforward—facing life straight on and not getting bogged down by negative characteristics. This does not mean having a stiff spine as opposed to being spineless. The stem of a rose is not rigid. I compare it to the flexible trunk of a willow tree which can survive a storm because it can go with the pressure of the wind while the hard, rigid oak can break in the same storm. It is not a matter of having enough will to bend or resist; it is where we choose to apply the large amount of will that we do have. This is where discrimination comes in.

Let your spine be straight. If you can walk straight with your head erect, that means there is nothing that you have to hide. The posture of your body, or even of a child's body, indicates a great deal. A child, already worried for whatever reasons, will slump in a chair, shoulders stooped, staring at the ground. It is no use to tell this child to sit up straight because the slumping is not the problem: it is the symptom. Watch people walking. How do they move? Very few are really straight and direct.

Cooperation implies at least some surrender. But even thoughts of surrender create anxiety in me. Sometimes I think I've governed my life according to one cardinal rule: resist everything. Yet resistance does have a place. I can think of it this way: I need to resist anything that tries to take me away from the Light.

Leaves will turn in any direction necessary to receive the light they need. Am I willing to do the same for what I need? What do I feed my mind? How do I use will and surrender together to serve my ideals? It does take surrender to let go, and yet the decision to let go is an act of directed will. I can see that surrender of my grudges and resentments would make space available in my mind for something far more useful.

—Swami Gopalananda

Leaves

— Swami Radha

Everything has its season. At the Ashram July is the month when the roses bloom. In time, everything comes to flower, even your love. The seed already contains the rose. Eventually, after the seed germinates, the first two leaves appear. The second pair of leaves is more refined than the first, and as the plant grows the ascending leaves become more and more refined until finally the flower appears. Slowly the flower unfolds, taking its own time, seeming to sense when the conditions are right. The plant has to work to produce the stem, the leaves, and the flower. Cause and effect are all around us. From the seed to the first pair of coarse leaves then finally to the flower—we can observe a process of evolution in miniature.

The process of evolution is around you and in you, and you cannot exclude yourself from it. Is it possible, then, for you to cooperate with this process of evolution? Yes. The power of choice is definitely yours. If you cooperate with the process of evolution as it pertains to you as an individual, your life will go considerably more smoothly. If you do not cooperate, knowing that you have a choice, then destiny can very easily take you by the neck and shake you to the bone, and there is ample evidence that this is what happens. On the other hand, many people can achieve something important in life only when they are put under great pressure. Without the pressure they do not exert the effort. The choice, however, *is* yours. You don't have to be shaken.

–swami radha–

Someone has removed the thorns. What an intriguing irony to have the potential for injury, even death, in something as attractive and enticing as a rose. Is it possible that the most beautiful in life can only be had through some kind of sacrifice? Attachment is a great obstacle to Liberation, I can see that. I also see that the ego must be sacrificed in order to realize the Most High. The pearl does, indeed, have its price. I can see that the pleasures and gifts of love that have come to me in this life must somehow be brought into balance through the pain of sacrifice. I don't think I would know how to experience gratitude otherwise.

—Swami Gopalananda

Thorns

—Swami Radha

The rose, as beautiful as it is, has something else besides the beauty. Thorns. If you try to grab the rose, the beauty of life, you may be hurt. The thorn is also symbolic for the ego and the mind sticking out from beneath the beauty and the soul. However, you can use the thorn to remove the thorn. If you want to know yourself and be free, you can use mind to investigate mind. You can use your selfishness constructively and investigate yourself using the process of reflection. Reflect on the events of your day, and if you are not satisfied, make changes. This is very different from judging and condemning yourself. Being overly critical is just as bad as not being critical at all. Proper criticism can come in your reflection with straight thinking—you find the facts and you deal with them as best you can so that you can rest assured in yourself. Reflection is a wonderful means for making the conscience clear.

I have a beautiful old picture of a person sitting on a lotus, holding a long-handled mirror. The picture is saying something about reflection. How does my face reflect in the mirror? Do I see a face of kindness, or greed and jealousy? Do I see a face that is trustworthy? Do my eyes reflect God's light or do they anxiously seek recognition? A reflection that is done daily means asking, "How have I passed this day and how can I learn from the possible mistakes of this day?" Learning means seeing what is, which requires going beyond condemnation and judgement. We learn by trial and error; in fact, all great things in life have been achieved by trial and error. The only real sin in life may be the intentional repetition of mistakes once they have been seen. To help reinforce our sincerity, we can offer the thorns to the Divine as we remove them, asking that it be the Divine who removes all the thorns from our life.

I have always removed the thorns from the roses that were to be used in a Rose Ceremony. When some people commented about this I said, "I'm not Divine Mother, but I hope even in this gesture that I can help remove some of the thorns from your life so that you won't be wounded by all of them." You can do the same for others. Whenever you give someone a gift of roses, take the thorns off beforehand with the thought that this is what you wish in your heart for the one to whom you are giving the gift.

Gradually, as I remove each petal, the centre is revealed. Even though it is still attached to the stem, still connected to the body of the rose, it is also meant to represent something other than the rose—living in the world but not of the world. The petals, the scent, the beautiful visible qualities of the rose emanate from the centre, which represents the essence of the flower. The essence sustains all that is visible and beautiful. I pick up the scissors to free the essence from the stem and suddenly the seriousness of what I am about to do becomes clear. Am I ready to give up my attachments? Do I even know what that means? How can I dedicate myself to something I cannot even see? Maybe if I let go of that attachment, a little room will be made for the Divine to help. Yes, that's the place to start.

—*Swami Gopalananda*

Centre—The Essence
—Swami Radha

If you decide to put the centre of the rose into the water, that can be seen as a dedication of all you are to the Most High, and I want to emphasize that that is what you surrender to. All the initiation ceremonies of the East are never meant to be a dedication of one human being to another; they are meant only to bring you into contact with the divinity within yourself and help you to take the last steps to Liberation. My initiations— Mantra, Brahmacharya, and Sanyas, were not a promise to my Guru. The obligation between my own Guru and me is only to support each other where possible.

It is a tough decision to dedicate yourself completely to the Divine because you know that it's serious and it carries a lot of weight. However, once you have dedicated yourself to the Most High, you have a destination in life and you are no longer caught like a leaf bouncing on the waves of life—here, there, and everywhere and not belonging anywhere. You have a destination and a means to get there, and that is the beginning of your path of Liberation. All actions in the Rose Ceremony will have a lasting impression if you are sincere.

—swami radha—

May I be as clear and transparent as this bowl,
and may my mind become as still and receptive
as the water it contains. May my eyes reflect the
Light just as these crystal facets reflect the Light of
the Temple. May my speech be a reflection of the
Wisdom that I have gained on this path.
Now I offer to the water all that keeps me apart.
May the water absorb these opposites floating on
the surface, and through the power of Light,
dissolve the pain of my separation into the
realization of divine love.

—Swami Gopalananda

Water and the Crystal Bowl
—Swami Radha

Placing the rose petals and the centre of the rose into the bowl of water is an act of surrender. Water can be associated with cleanliness and purification, the water of life. You surrender to the water of life, and this is all beautifully symbolized by your intent and your actions in the Rose Ceremony. The water becomes holy through this concentration of intent and also by chanting the Mantra. Overnight the pairs of opposites become purified, and in the morning this water will be distributed. After the Rose Ceremony you are still a human being who has to struggle along the path, using discrimination and doing the best you can at any given moment. To remove yourself from the pair of opposites represented by punishment and reward is a tremendous undertaking. But as you begin, you will find that

God's grace supports you, and if you put forward even a little effort, you will become aware of how readily available that grace is to you.

The scissors you use to cut the stem can remind you of your power of discrimination, the power to cut off the ego. In everything you do in life, you should use as much discrimination as you can. Think things through and you won't make too many mistakes.

–swami radha–

Earlier today I took the petals out of the bowl of water to give them time to dry a little. It's good to be back in my sacred place again. It feels different from yesterday; I feel so much lighter and I don't quite know why. We're chanting a different Mantra, this one to Lord Siva. Siva, the Destroyer. He's really more a creator—creating new possiblities with the energy that's been released from the chain of grudges and resentments. I'll be glad to burn this list; it was a little startling to see how tightly I was hanging on to old resentments—skeletons that should have been left in the cremation ground long ago. Lord Siva will use the ashes to protect Himself from the blazing sun. Memory.

—Swami Gopalananda

Fire
—Swami Radha

Mind has an awesome power, and if that power is bound up in long-held grudges and simmering resentment, then the road to Liberation is simply closed. Fire, which is symbolic for light, wisdom, and passion, also destroys the ignorance that fosters grudges and resentment.

If the power of the mind is given to an ego that constantly seeks changes and schemes for self-gratification, such a mind is considered to be impure. A teacher in the East does not think of the one who has never made a mistake as having a pure mind. No. One who has sufficient awareness to live by his or her own highest ideals and ethics and who maintains that awareness through daily reflection and introspection is approaching the state of pure mind. Through the power of mind, human beings are co-creators with God.

When we become aware of our own grudges and resentments, it is useful to remember that there are lots of people who may have plenty of reason to hold grudges and resentments against us. We, too, have created the circumstances. The Rose Ceremony presents an opportunity to free yourself from the chain of attachment that is forged through your resentment toward another. Yoga is the path of Liberation, and it's a glorious path for anyone who understands what is required to be free. If your choices in life are always determined by the ego, then you'll miss the entire purpose of this lifetime. Some pleasure is not only justified; some pleasure is acceptable and right. But a life of selfishness is a great tragedy. If the ego is allowed to grab all the power that comes from prayer, then the serpent of wisdom becomes the serpent of evil caught in an endless round of temptation. Wisdom or temptation, the power of choice is there for every individual.

In the temples in India, all the rose petals are collected for burning in the temple fire. As long as you live between punishment and reward and the resulting myriad of opposites, you don't have divine wisdom. Put some petals into the fire along with your paper listing your grudges and resentments, with the understanding that ignorance, living in the realm of the opposites, is burned in the fire of divine wisdom.

And you must not take the grudges and resentments back. You are offering these things to the Most High in return for divine love, and that offering is like a promise. You must keep your promises, whether they are made to another person or whether they are in the form of a dedication of your own life to the spiritual path. But the most serious promises to break are those you make to the Most High.

If you feel that you are sincere at the time, and the temptation of resentment comes back, then resort to prayer. Put yourself into the Light and ask that your own mind, your heart, and your emotions be illuminated sufficiently to let go. To the degree that you can let go of your resentments and your grudges, you will be set free. That is what you have to remember. That is what the Rose Ceremony is all about.

> The cremation ground
> is the place of the heart.
> In the ashes of my illusions
> I found truth.

Swami Radha had the courage and strength of character to speak only to my potential. She challenged me to build self-respect by putting quality into my work. Her first measure of quality was sincerity of effort. She cared so much for her students that she could speak only to the ideals in each of us. She was, in the full sense of the term, a Guru.

Self-respect carries with it an enduring sweetness. How could I ever repay the one who has shown me the way into a life of purpose, who has given me life itself?

—Swami Gopalananda

Prasad

—Swami Radha

Divine wisdom is sweetness because it takes away the bitterness of life. Through divine wisdom you learn to see the other side of life, not just the pain. When the bitterness is removed you can experience the inherent sweetness in life. The sweet is called prasad. In giving prasad, the Guru gives you a promise: to share everything with you that he or she knows, to help you and further you on your spiritual path.

Conclusion

Swami Radha

My Guru cleared the way for me, but even if I had a million dollars I could never pay him back. Because of Gurudev, my life suddenly made sense and was worth living. I can pay him back only by helping others.

You are here for the same thing. If you want to be helped, you can be helped. But your obligation in return is to help others.

There are events that are unpredictable

But some are very obvious.

The powers of decision

in the unseen

are hard to recognize.

When will it happen?

Why does it happen?

Destiny will fight hard

before it yields its mystery.

–swami radha–